Stoicism

The Stoic Way of Life in a Modern World

Free membership into the Mastermind Self Development Group!

For a limited time, you can join the Mastermind Self Development Group for free! You will receive videos and articles from top authorities in self development as well as a special group only offers on new books and training programs. There will also be a monthly member only draw that gives you a chance to win any book from your Kindle wish list!

If you sign up through this link
<http://www.mastermindselfdevelopment.com/specialreport> you will also get a special free report on the Wheel of Life. This report will give you a visual look at your current life and then take you through a series of exercises that will help you plan what your perfect life looks like. The workbook does not end there; we then take you through a process to help you plan how to achieve that perfect life. The process is very powerful and has the potential to change your life forever. Join the group now and start to change your life!
<http://www.mastermindselfdevelopment.com/specialreport>

Table of Contents

Introduction

Chapter 1: The Basics

Chapter 2: Application

Chapter 3: Moving Forward

Conclusion

© Copyright 2017 by Mastermind Self Development All rights reserved.

The transmission, duplication or reproduction of any of the following work including specific information will be considered an illegal act irrespective of if it is done electronically or in print. This extends to creating a secondary or tertiary copy of the work or a recorded copy and is only allowed with express written consent of the Publisher. All additional right reserved.

The information in the following pages is broadly considered to be a truthful and accurate account of facts and as such any inattention, use or misuse of the information in question by the reader will render any resulting actions solely under their purview. There are no scenarios in which the publisher or the original author of this work can be in any fashion deemed liable for any hardship or damages that may befall them after undertaking information described herein.

Additionally, the information in the following pages is intended only for informational purposes and should thus be thought of as universal. As befitting its nature, it is presented without assurance regarding its prolonged validity or interim quality. Trademarks that are mentioned are done without written consent and can in no way be considered an endorsement from the trademark holder.

The author of this book has taken careful measures to share vital information about the subject. May its readers acquire the right knowledge, wisdom, inspiration, and succeed.

Introduction

Congratulations on downloading this book and thank you for doing so.

The following chapters will teach you everything that you need to learn about Stoicism. It is worth noting that Stoicism is not just a body of rules and principles. True Stoicism is a way of life.

Chapter 1 discusses the basics so that you will have a good foundation of what Stoicism really is.

Chapter 2 talks about the different teachings of Stoicism, and how you can apply them in your day-to-day life. After all, the spirit of Stoicism lies in actual practice.

Chapter 3 gives encouragements and suggestions on how to make the philosophy and practice of Stoicism more alive in your life. If you think that you already know what you need to know about Stoicism, then it is time to take it to the next level.

There are plenty of books on this subject on the market, thanks again for choosing this one! Every effort was made to ensure it is full of as much useful information as possible. Please enjoy!

Chapter 1: The Basics

Before you dive into the teachings of Stoicism, it is best to first establish a good foundation of the basics of Stoicism. The basics are important because they form the fundamentals of this philosophical way of life.

Brief history

Long ago, back in 301 BC, one of the great philosophers at that time, Zeno, taught at the Stoa Poikile. This is, in fact, where Stoicism got its name. Unlike other philosophers, Zeno taught openly in public. The roots of Stoicism can be traced as far back in the time of the renowned philosopher, Socrates. This is because the ideas of Zeno were influenced by the Cynics, the founding father of which had been a disciple of Socrates.

Scholars normally classify Stoicism into 3 phases:

- Early Stoa
- Middle Stoa
- Late Stoa

It is worth noting that no surviving work has survived from the first two phases (Early and Middle Stoa), only the works from the Late Stoa in Roman texts have survived.

What is Stoicism?

Stoicism is a school of Hellenistic philosophy. It primarily deals with personal ethics. It is worth noting that for the Stoics, the study of philosophy is not just something that you read or talk about as a pastime hobby. Rather, the Stoics consider philosophy as a way of life. It is something that you put into action. Stoicism seeks to transform negative emotions into positive ones. This, in a way, mimics the art of the ancient Hermeticism whereby negative energies are transformed into positive ones.

In many respects, Stoicism has many similarities with the teachings of Buddhism, specifically those that came from Siddhartha Gautama Buddha. For the Stoics, it is important to live virtuously and reasonably. According to the Stoics, living with virtue and reason is the way to live in harmony with the divine universe. It is worth noting that true Stoicism does not rely on mere claims and arguments, but finds its meaning in actual application. It also teaches one to be unbiased and not be affected by external things. Simply put, Stoicism teaches people to be a better human being. It is a way of happiness founded upon right knowledge and actual practice.

Seneca

Lucius Annaeus Seneca was a Stoic philosopher. He was a statesman, philosopher, adviser, and a writer. He was raised in Rome where he first learned the science and art of philosophy and rhetoric. His works covered various topics, such as friendship, moral obligation, humility, and self-awareness, among others.

Epictetus

Epictetus came from a humble origin. He was born as a slave. He had a strong passion for philosophy and learned from a master, Gaius Musonius Rufus. He started to teach philosophy in Rome after Nero's death. He then moved and taught in Greece where he founded a school of philosophy to teach Stoicism. This leads another prominent figure in Stoicism, Marcus Aurelius, who was a student of Epictetus.

Marcus Aurelius

Considered today as one of the greatest Roman emperors, he wrote a journal called as *Meditations*. This book has served even today as reminders of the Stoic principles. Its primary focus is on humility, nature, self-awareness, and death, among others.

It is worth noting that none of the three heralds of Stoicism had a big audience. Therefore, their reputation as far as their teachings are concerned is quite a mystery. Seneca became known in the 17th century, but he was totally forgotten in the late 19th century. By then, the popularity of Stoic teachers alternated between Marcus Aurelius and Epictetus.

It is also worth noting that the Meditations of Marcus Aurelius, which is referred to time and time again in this book, was not meant to be a public book or document. It is a journal made only for Marcus Aurelius. The journal contains his day-to-day reflections. With regard to the writings of Epictetus, it is worth noting that although they are attributed as written by Epictetus, they were actually written by Arrian, his disciple. Seneca was well conscious that he repeated almost the same teachings several times. He did defend himself by saying that "he does but inculcate over and over the same counsels to those that over and over commit the same faults."

There is no such thing as to the best teacher or philosopher of Stoicism. They all laid down wonderful teachings and foundation, and people have different tastes. Hence, no one can claim that Epictetus is better than Marcus Aurelius or that Seneca is the best among the three. After all, even during their time, they did not compete as to who will have the most popular name in the world of Stoicism.

Basic tenets

The Stoics classified the study of philosophy into three:

- Logic
- Monistic physics
- Naturalistic ethics

It is worth noting that their primary focus is on ethics. According to the Stoics, fortitude and self-control are needed in order to overcome destructive emotions. When one is unbiased and if his mind is free from thoughts of prejudice and preferences, only then can he realize the universal reason, also known as logos. To the Stoics, it is important to improve a person's ethical and moral well-being. Stoics strive to be "free from anger, envy, and jealousy," and they also give importance to equality to the point that slaves must be considered as equals of all other men like themselves on the reasoning that human beings are "products of nature."

To the Stoics, everything is material. Words, ideas, principles, emotions, and others are all material since they all manifest in the physical plane. For example, when someone is happy, it manifests in the way he laughs or smiles. Ideas are also followed by appropriate actions. Emotions, of course, are easily expressed. To them, even God is manifested in nature. Even the mind and the soul are material. From the mind, impressions are created, which are then transferred to the soul. And, from the soul, movements are produced in the material world. As you can notice, the invisible manifests itself in visible forms.

Like other schools of philosophy, knowledge is something that is considered valuable for the Stoics. According to them, a certainty of knowledge is possible through the use of right reasons. Of course, like the Socratic method, knowledge has to be validated and stand the test of reasoning with one's peers, as well as the collective judgment of everyone.

The Stoics also believe in the oneness of everything. To them, the whole world is one and that the divine energy permeates all things. This is the same as other more popular beliefs and spiritual traditions. Everything is interconnected, but there is always a space for one to exercise his free will.

Is it for you?

It bears stressing that Stoicism is not a religion. It does not belong to any particular sect or tradition. Rather, it is a way of life. As such, it is open to everyone. Anyone can be a Stoic. You can be a Stoic. All that you need is to learn its teachings and apply them in your everyday life.

It does not matter whether you are rich or poor. It does not matter whether you have a job or not. You can be a Stoic if you choose to. The good news is that regardless what your status in life may be, there is always something wonderful to learn about Stoicism that can have a strong and positive impact on your life.

Stoicism vs. the modern world

When people talk about Stoicism, most of them cannot help but feel as if they are taken back in ancient time, as if Stoicism were something that only belongs to history. However, it is worth noting that even though the great philosophers and teachers of Stoicism have long passed away, their teachings and ideas have survived the test of time. After all, the true spirit of Stoicism does not rely on ancient books or manuscripts; it lives in the hearts and minds of the people, in the ideas and principles that do not die. Whether you come from eons ago or part of the modern world with all its technological innovations, Stoicism lives.

Stoicism was built for difficult times. It was made in a time of great crisis when wars were waged by different empires and groups. The modern world is not far from this. In fact, the world today as you know it appears to be getting more difficult to deal with. There are more people today who are stressed out and unhappy with their lives than centuries ago.

Although the philosophy of the Stoics does not guarantee any happiness in the afterlife, it lays down a way for one to be happy in this lifetime, without having to depend on the uncertainty of the next life, if any. Stoicism understands that happiness cannot depend on things that can easily be altered. Even if you have a successful career today, it does not guarantee that you will remain successful after five years. You may have millions in your bank accounts right now, but a simple disaster can take all those money away from you. Your loved ones may change, and they may no longer be with you tomorrow. These things are all outside of your control. However, to the Stoics, there is a place that no one can take away from you, and it is your inner self. If you can learn to conquer your inner self, then external events and things cannot harm you. You can always decide to be happy, to be brave and reasonable. You will have an unshakable happiness that no one can take away from you.

According to Epictetus, "Where is the good? In the will…If anyone is unhappy, let him remember that he is unhappy by reason of himself alone." You should not search for happiness outside of yourself. The happiness that you seek is all inside you.

It is also worth noting that Christianity has a strong Stoic influence. In fact, long ago, Stoic leaders were also Christians. Although Christianity may downplay any resemblance or similarities with Stoicism, it cannot be denied that the soul of Stoicism can be found in some of the fundamental teachings of Christianity.

Whether you are engaged in business or simply want to develop good leadership qualities, then you can also find encouragement and strength from Stoicism. There are many leadership qualities displayed by the former U.S. President Barack Obama, and even those of Bill Clinton, that resemble Stoic teachings and qualities.

In fact, it is not a secret that one of Clinton's most favorite books is the *Meditations* of Marcus Aurelius.

Of course, as long as life exists and humanity walks on the face of this planet, then the spirit of Stoicism will continue to live. So long as men seek for happiness in this ever-changing world, Stoicism will continue to exist.

Stoicism vs. Buddhism

There are certain similarities between Stoicism and Buddhism, such as giving importance to the present moment and not seeking happiness outside of one's self; however, it is worth noting that they also have some notable differences. First and foremost, Buddhism is a religion, while Stoicism is a way of life. Hence, anyone can be a Stoic, as long as the person is willing to learn and practice the teachings of Stoicism.

Buddhism also does not believe in a creator, such as a God, while Stoics believe in the existence of God to the point that God's existence is manifested in the physical world. The Buddhists also believe in karma and reincarnation, while Stoics do not believe in such, and views death as a normal part of the world. Also, in Buddhism, each time you save an animal from being slaughtered, you will receive a good karma in return. Such belief has no place in Stoicism.

Although with some differences, it is worth noting that their core values and principles are the same or almost the same — and this is the important part. They both encourage that man should not seek too much of material wealth and glory but should strive to improve one's mind and spirit. Whether a Stoic or a Buddhist, you should know that the mind is a crucial element of the key to happiness. The goal of every Buddhist to achieve nirvana or ultimate happiness is also similar to the goal of a Stoic to achieve apatheia or a peaceful state of mind that does not cling to either pleasure or suffering in order to be happy.

Chapter 2: Application

The best way to learn Stoicism is to learn its teachings and apply them in your everyday life. After all, true Stoicism is not just about gaining knowledge, but more importantly, it exists in actual application. You do not become a Stoic simply by reading books, not even by memorizing the principles of this philosophical school. It is when you live the ideas and teachings of Stoicism that one becomes a true Stoic.

Oneness of spirituality

Just a wave must realize that it is not just a wave but the ocean, so you should realize that you are not different from one another. You are your friend and your enemy. Hence, you should strive to help people and do good to those who are kind to you, and even to those who are not. You must not see yourself separate from them. Also, Stoicism is not a religion, but it teaches that all religions are one. Just like in Hinduism and Paganism, they believe in many gods and goddess, yet also believe in the oneness of life and spirituality, and that God is one and inseparable.

The oneness of spirituality shows itself like a web of life. It teaches the oneness of life, and how a single action or gesture can have an influence upon the whole. As a human being, Stoicism teaches that you should see others to be not different from yourself. This oneness of spirituality also resounds the words of Jesus Christ: "Love your neighbor as yourself." There is no division, only unity and oneness.

"Constantly regard the universe as one living being, having one substance and one soul; and observe how all things have reference to one perception, the perception of this one living being; and how all things act with one movement; and how all things are the cooperating causes of all things that exist; observe too the continuous spinning of the thread and the structure of the web." —Marcus Aurelius

Live the moment of Now

An important teaching in Stoicism is to experience and live the present moment. Unfortunately, today, many people are busy with their day-to-day life that they fail to truly exist in the present moment. Most are unconscious of what they are doing and act as if they were robots merely letting time pass them by. For the Stoics, one should enjoy the present moment and not worry about the future. This is in line with a teaching in Buddhism that says, "If you can solve your problems, what is the use of worrying? If you cannot solve your problems, what is the use of worrying?"

Of course, this does not mean that you will no longer try to think or solve your problems. Rather, you can give time to ponder about your problems, but after such moment, you must control yourself to focus again on the present time and enjoy it as much as you can. Do not let yourself and your mind to exist in the future or in the past.

Let us say, for example, you enter into a business deal and you do not know whether it will turn out good or bad. To the Stoics, instead of worrying whether or not it will have a positive outcome, you should enjoy what you have and do things to make it work instead of worrying.

Many people fail to live in the present moment. This seems to be the most common thing that happens every day. People have gotten stuck in a routine that they are no longer conscious of what is truly happening in the present moment. They fail to feel and realize the miracles that exist in their day-to-day life. As the saying goes, "Stop and smell the roses." It is very easy to get caught up in your work or everyday tasks; however, it is important that let yourself exist in the moment of Now and experience its miracles. Life is beautiful, and every moment is precious. If you do not feel the beauty of every passing moment, then it is a sign that you should, indeed, "Stop and smell the roses."

"True happiness is to enjoy the present, without anxious dependence upon the future, not to amuse ourselves with either hopes or fears but to rest satisfied with what we have, which is sufficient, for he that is so wants nothing. The greatest blessings of mankind are within us and within our reach. A wise man is content with his lot, whatever it may be, without wishing for what he has not." —Seneca

"Nothing, to my way of thinking, is a better proof of a well ordered mind than a man's ability to stop just where he is and pass some time in his own company." — Seneca, Letters From a Stoic

"It's ruinous for the soul to be anxious about the future and miserable in advance of misery, engulfed by anxiety that the things it desires might remain its own until the very end. For such a soul will never be at rest — by longing for things to come it will lose the ability to enjoy present things."— Seneca, Moral Letters

Live a virtuous life

There are four cardinal virtues in Stoicism:

- Wisdom
- Courage
- Self-control
- Justice

These areas map out an entire human experience. Taken together, they are about living a whole life as a human being. According to the Stoics, men should live with virtue. Take note that to the Stoics, virtue is not just a body of knowledge, but it also shapes one's desires and emotions. A change or development in one's virtue can create a positive impact on a person's life. The Stoics believe that every person has, in some sense, already has virtue ingrained in himself. However, there is a need to develop this virtue. To develop this virtue, you will need to have the right understanding and to apply this virtue to yourself and others. To the Stoics, it is through the application of virtue or living a virtuous life that is necessary to achieve true happiness. It is also with the exercise of virtue that a Stoic can remain happy even in the difficult of times. Of course, this level is not easy to achieve. It takes practice and a well-developed sense of virtue to be able to keep one's happiness unshakable. The good news is that Stoicism makes this possible.

Of course, it is important for you to learn the virtue to follow. According to the teachings of Stoicism, you should turn to those things that have a positive quality, such as love, justice, compassion, courage, and self-control, among others. It is also taught that you should avoid those things that are negative in nature and are valueless. Once you stumble upon the path and tread a wrong or sinful path, then that is the time that you will have inner conflicts, which will destroy your inner peace and happiness. Hence, it is of utmost importance that you live a virtuous life.

In the modern world, it is easy to be misled by strange teachings and tempting offers. For example, in order to achieve quick gains, one can simply sell prohibited drugs. However, this is not the path to happiness, as according to the Stoics; for even if you gain material things, you will not be happy unless you live a truly virtuous life.

"He who is making progress has learned that desire is for things good and that aversion is for things evil, and further, that peace and calm are only achieved as a man gets the things he wants and avoids the things he doesn't want. Since virtue is rewarded with happiness, calm and serenity, progress towards virtue is progress towards its benefits and this progress is always a step towards perfection." —*Epictetus*

Take care of your thoughts

Stoicism teaches that you should be careful of the thoughts that you entertain in your mind. The thoughts that you have in your mind have a strong impact on your mood and your life. Unfortunately, the modern world is used to the idea that thoughts are just thoughts, and that they do not have any physical manifestation or effect. To the Stoics, thoughts are just as real as objects, so you must be careful with the thoughts that you have in your mind.

In the modern world, there is the principle of positive thinking. The same applies in Stoicism where you are encouraged to think only nice and beautiful thoughts, as well as to stay away from those thoughts that have a negative nature. In real life, instead of complaining and thinking just how poor you are, you should instead think of ways to make money, or more specifically, the positive actions that you can take to be better.

Thoughts can be either good or bad, positive or negative. You need to discipline your mind to think more of positive thoughts. This may not be easy, especially when life takes a hard turn against you, but with practice, hard work, and dedication to living a virtuous life, this is possible. Therefore, strive to work on having more positive thoughts. Instead of thinking that you cannot succeed in life or work, tell yourself that you can do it and that there is no obstacle that you cannot overcome. If you continue to exercise the habit of only thinking about positive things, you will feel happier and be a more positive person. However, if you do the opposite, life will tend to be very stressful. Control your thoughts; control your life.

The happiness of your life depends upon the quality of your thoughts. —Marcus Aurelius

Do not let other people's thoughts make you change who you are

Many people these days live a life that is not of their own choosing. The influence and demands of society are so strong that people many fail to be who they truly are. It is important that you do not be like them. Never worry about what other people may think about you. As long as you stay in the path of virtue, you will always be blameless.

This, of course, does not mean that you should ignore the opinions of others. Instead, just consider them as suggestions and nothing more. You are always free to do the opposite of what the whole world may think. If you keep a good heart and exercise righteousness and virtue in every step, then there is nothing for you to worry about. For example, I know a man who has always dreamed of being a writer. However, the path that was set for him was to be a lawyer. After all, lawyers are usually held with the highest respects. He yielded into the dictates and perceptions of the people around him, and he became a lawyer. However, it cannot be denied that even today, he is not happy as a lawyer, but only as a writer. Happiness is within you. Do not let people tell you how to be happy. What people think matters less. Not to mention, most people are good at giving opinions but do not know how to observe them themselves. A good way to live a sad and stressful life is to be too concerned about what other people think. Do not forget that if they truly love you, they will respect whatever decision you make. However, if they do not really love you, there will always be something to criticize about you despite doing everything that you ever do. Hence, although it is good to think of others, you should not neglect to think of yourself, too.

But, if you do not listen to other people, how do you know how to act properly? According to Seneca, you need to listen to your conscience. This is another reason why man needs to live a virtuous life; otherwise, even his conscience may get clouded, which can prevent him from making just decisions.

I have often wondered how it is that every man loves himself more than all the rest of men, but yet sets less value on his own opinions of himself than on the opinions of others. —Marcus Aurelius

Be satisfied and happy with what you have

Stoics know that true happiness is inside every human being. One does not need to look for happiness in some distant future or long-forgotten land. It is here, right now, in you.

Happiness is possible. This is so, especially if you know how to appreciate the real value of what you have, such as the happiness of being alive and being loved. However, many people take things for granted. Most have to first lose the things that they love before they see their value. This is considered a terrible mistake that is close to stupidity. Unfortunately, such is normal in life, especially in the modern world. Long ago, people knew the importance of every moment, especially during the times when kingdoms were at war and there was always the possibility of death or dying in everyday life. It is worth noting that even today, the same principle or lesson applies. After all, one does not need the impending existence of death before he should realize the value or meaning of his life. The Stoics are so focused on this teaching to the point that they contemplate the idea of death. They imagine and think about losing everything that they love. This way, they get to more appreciate their value. You can do this on your own. Give yourself some time to reflect. Now, imagine your loved ones. Imagine that they have just died. How do you feel? Take note that such occurrence has a possibility to happen at any time. After all, accidents do happen. Ponder and reflect about what is truly meaningful in your life. If you realize that you give your loved ones less than you should, then now is the time to make the necessary adjustments. If only you realize the meaning or value of what you have right now, then you would be grateful at every hour and every minute. Just the fact that you are still alive is a wonderful joy. Use it wisely.

He is a wise man who does not grieve for the things which he has not, but rejoices for those which he has. —Epictetus

To control your emotions, look within

Stoicism puts emphasis on overcoming destructive emotions. Most people these days are led by their emotions instead of being in control of them. You should know that emotions exist within. It is true that external factors or events can influence how you feel; however, it is also true that the home of emotions lies within you. An emotion can only manifest itself if you allow it to.

For example, if you are feeling down and lonely, you can feel the emotion inside you. However, you can overcome it by placing your focus on something that is positive, something that is fun for you. When you do this, the emotion will tend to dissipate on its own. Take note that there are two kinds of emotion: positive and negative. Of course, if it is a positive or pleasurable emotion, then that is something that you should enjoy to the fullest. However, if you are faced with a negative emotion, remind yourself that you have a choice whether or not you want to be affected by it.

"Today I escaped anxiety. Or no, I discarded it, because it was within me, in my own perceptions — not outside." —Marcus Aurelius, Meditations

Choose your friends wisely

Stick to those who have a positive outlook in life and are striving to be the best that they can be. It is good to be with people who have a strong and positive mindset, and avoid those that give no respect or meaning to life. Be careful with whom you associate with, especially those that you get to spend time with on a regular basis. In business, they have a saying which goes like this: "You are the average of the five people around you." The people around you have a strong impact on your personality and on your life. Of course, it is still up to you to decide whether or not you will allow them to change who you are, and if the change would be for the better or the worse. Be with those of good company, and avoid people who are loud and boisterous, for they are vexations to the spirit. If you stick to those who are kind and good, it will be much easier for you to love kindly as well. Hence, in choosing your friends, it is a good to exercise some caution. If possible, choose those that have a higher spiritual or philosophical development than yourself.

"Choose someone whose way of life as well as words, and whose very face as mirroring the character that lies behind it, have won your approval. Be always pointing him out to yourself either as your guardian or as your model. This is a need, in my view, for someone as a standard against which our characters can measure themselves. Without a ruler to do it against you won't make the crooked straight." —Seneca, Letters From a Stoic

Put your knowledge into practice

For the Stoics, acquiring knowledge alone is not enough. The true meaning and spirit of Stoicism lie in actual practice. Yes, it is good to read books and develop your intellectual understanding of Stoicism; however, one does not become a Stoic simply by reading and memorizing all the books and articles on Stoicism. It is only through actual practice that you can be a Stoic. You should be able to live its principles and teachings in your everyday life.

For example, by now you already have a good insight of what Stoicism is; however, this is not enough. You need to apply and live what you know.

"Don't just say you have read books. Show that through them you have learned to think better, to be a more discriminating and reflective person. Books are the training weights of the mind. They are very helpful, but it would be a bad mistake to suppose that one has made progress simply by having internalized their contents." Epictetus, The Art of Living

Make every moment count

In poetry, there is a saying, "carpe diem" or seize the day. Stoics realize the value and meaning of every moment, and they would not allow having a single moment be wasted. Many people these days seem to wait for the right and perfect moment to love their life, without realizing that that moment is the here and now. Do not postpone what you can do today to another day. If you can do an act of kindness at this moment, why wait and delay it tomorrow? Be a good at all times. The good news is that every moment is an opportunity for you to do something nice. In Buddhism, there is a teaching with regard to the contemplation of death. If you think and imagine that you would die today, what would you do? Do not wait for the angel of death to come knocking at your door because, by then, it will be too late. As according to the words of Morrie: "Learn how to live and you will learn how to die. Learn how to die and you will learn how to live." Do not forget that every moment is a miracle. Make it count.

"Not to live as if you had endless years ahead of you. Death overshadows you. While you're alive and able — be good." —Marcus Aurelius, Meditations

Discipline of assent

People usually give in to strong impulses. This is also the way they lose control and get led by their emotions. According to the Stoic's discipline of assent, you need to not allow yourself to get carried away regardless of how strong an impulse may be. Instead of allowing it to dictate your course of action, you should learn to postpone your reaction and simply regard the impulse or temptation as something that is separate from you, which city actually is. This way, you will be able to control it, and you can decide whether or not you will give in to the impulse or not. True Stoics do not allow themselves to be controlled by feelings. They see them as separate and can be controlled. Hence, in order to minimize the power of an impulse, you can simply delay reacting to it.

It is worth noting, however, that this is not easy to do. There are simply many impulses or emotions that are not easy to control or "postpone," such as anger or jealousy. However, with practice, these things can be put under your control. According to Epictetus, the key here is the moment when you are deciding. Instead of allowing yourself to just go with the flow and allow someone or something to dictate your action, you should learn to postpone your response. Simply lapse for a moment and think it through with a clear mind. Again, do not expect this to be easy. However, just keep on practicing it, and will soon have better control of your emotions and even your thoughts.

There's usually a moment — however brief — when you decide to give in to an impulse or resist it. You have a choice. But you agree to act out that script you've performed 1000 times, even though it always has lousy consequences.

"Hold on a moment; let me see who you are and what you represent. Let me put you to the test." —Epictetus, Discourses and Selected Writings

Replace bad habits with good ones

According to the Stoics, the way to combat bad habits is not to focus on removing a particular bad habit. Instead, you should work on cultivating the opposite quality, which is presumably positive in nature. For example, instead of trying to remove your fear, you need to work on building courage. You do not work on destroying your fear. The reason is that after removing the negative quality, you will still be left with nothing. This is the same as the ancient teaching in Heretics whereby to remove a particular quality, you simply have to develop its opposite quality. This is a very important teaching that can unlock the secrets to controlling and overcoming your moods and even your thoughts. Of course, this is not as easy as it sounds. Truly, it takes serious practice and dedication to be a real Stoic.

For example, let us say that you have an issue with being too lazy. Hence, laziness is the bad habit that you want to change. According to the Stoics, instead of complaining and coming up with a way to remove that laziness that you have, you should work on the opposite quality. Hence, if you are lazy with our studies in school, then it is time for you to spend more time studying. If you only study for an hour a day, then it is time to improve that study habit and make it at least 4 hours per day. It is important that you stick to this new routine. Yes, it will be quite uncomfortable and even difficult at first but you will soon get used to it. Soon, you will notice that you no longer deal with said laziness. You can apply the same principle to other parts of your life.

"What aid can we find to combat habit? The opposed habit... So if you like doing something, do it regularly; if you don't like doing something, make a habit of doing something different." —Epictetus

Reflect

The Stoics make time for reflection. They think and come up with ways to improve their life and their mind. A good way to do this is to think about your day before you sleep. Every night, when you are lying in bed, think about what happened during the day. Could you think of anything that you could have done better? If yes, know what it is and make the necessary adjustments. Make kg a habit to reflect on your life and seek for ways to be better.

By reflecting, you get to view yourself from a different perspective. You will have a much clearer view of yourself and your life. Be open to developments or improvements that you can do. Do not be afraid of making positive changes. Stoics know how to look back so that they will have more wisdom when they move forward.

"A key point to bear in mind: The value of attentiveness varies in proportion to its object. You're better off not giving the small things more time than they deserve." — Marcus Aurelius, Meditations

I will keep constant watch over myself and — most usefully — will put each day up for review. For this is what makes us evil — that none of us looks back upon our own lives. We reflect upon only that which we are about to do. And yet our plans for the future descend from the past. – Seneca, Moral Letters

You are halfway done!

Congratulations on making it to the halfway point of the journey. Many try and give up long before even getting to this point, so you are to be congratulated on this. You have shown that you are serious about getting better every day. I am also serious about improving my life, and helping others get better along the way. To do this I need your feedback. Click on the link below and take a moment to let me know how this book has helped you. If you feel there is something missing or something you would like to see differently, I would love to know about it. I want to ensure that as you and I improve, this book continues to improve as well. Thank you for taking the time to ensure that we are all getting the most from each other.

Love

The Stoics are aware that they have control over their actions, and that what they do usually affect how other people treat them. Let us admit the truth that everyone wants to be loved. According to the Stoics, if you want to be loved, then you do not need to wait for someone to do it for you. Instead, you can take the first step and start loving. The same applies to other parts of life. For example, if you want to be happy, then make someone happy. Remember the words of Jesus Christ: "Do unto others what you would want them to do unto you." This is considered as the golden rule. The same teaching and practice exist in Stoicism. It encourages everyone to love.

Of course, this is also not easy to do, especially when you do not receive love in return. However, the Stoics understand that true love is unconditional. It is not being loved that matters so much as you have loved. In fact, just the experience of loving, even without being loved in return, is one of the best things to experience in life. For the Stoics, anyone who desires to be loved must first learn how to love.

"If you would be loved, love." —Seneca

Do not let other people penetrate your mind

This is related to the teaching that you should guard your thoughts. It is easy to remember happy memories, and this is a good thing. However, it is also easy to keep bad memories in your mind. In fact, when people treat you badly or unjustly, it is common for people to spend lots of time replaying the bad experience in their mind. After all, you are only human. You can also get hurt. Although such reaction is normal, the Stoics know that they have a choice whether or not to allow such person to ruin their mood and make them feel bad. The thing is that by still thinking about the person or incident, you give the person power over you. This usually happens in the world. For example, let us say that you get verbally attacked. This can be irritating and can oftentimes hurt your feelings. However, if you keep on thinking about it or giving the offender some power by always thinking about him, you can lose your own happiness. Do not forget the other Stoic teaching that happiness depends on the quality of your thoughts. So, in such case, what you can do is to spend a short time to analyze what happened, make a decision on what to do, and then move on. Instead of simply reminiscing the negative memory, you should fill your mind with positive thoughts — thoughts of love and happiness — and enjoy life.

"If a person gave your body to any stranger he met on his way, you would certainly be angry. And do you feel no shame in handing over your own mind to be confused and mystified by anyone who happens to verbally attack you?" — Epictetus

Life is not too short

Okay, this might contradict other teachings and beliefs; but according to Seneca, man's idea of the shortness of life is a misconception. It is not that man is not given enough time to live his life and pursue his dreams; rather, people usually waste their time doing something else.

If there is anything that you want to do in life, then make time for it. Do not wait for the angel of death to come knocking at your door before you take action. Just the fact that you get to read this book means that you have some time in your hands. Yes, it may not be as much time as you would want because of your busy schedule — but there is still time nonetheless. This is also one of the reasons why it is good to ponder about death or dying. If you know that death is getting near, then you would tend not to delay anything. It is unfortunate that people usually put off things that they can already do. Instead of doing something meaningful, they tend to spend their time with things that have no or little value.

Take note that life is not short. You can do with life what you would want. However, time is still limited. Therefore, stop procrastinating and take action. If you have been delaying writing that dream book of yours or taking your family out for dinner, then now is the time to take action. You have time, and you need to spend it wisely.

"If a person gave your body to any stranger he met on his way, you would certainly be angry. And do you feel no shame in handing over your own mind to be confused and mystified by anyone who happens to verbally attack you?" — Seneca

Negative visualization

Although the Stoics teach that you should not think of negative things, there is an exception to the rule, and that is when you do negative visualization. According to Epictetus, when a parent kisses her child goodnight, she should also do so considering the possibility that her child might die during the night. According to the Stoics, you should remind yourself that there is a chance that you will not see each other again. This practice, of course, is not limited to kissing a child goodnight. There are many ways to come up with negative visualization. For example, you can imagine your house getting burned or losing your favorite dress. Of course, the point of this exercise is not to make you sad and ruin your mood. Rather, negative visualization has three purposes:

- By visualizing the worst that can happen, you are able to prepare for the misfortune. For example, let use the example of your home getting burned. You can now take action to prevent this from happening. You can also start installing your house with fire extinguishers.
- By using negative visualization, the effect of the misfortune will be less if ever it does occur. By doing this exercise, you get to prepare your mind and emotion for the worst.
- By contemplating that you will lose something, it will help you appreciate its value more fully. Unfortunately, many people have the bad habit of

taking things for granted. They think that they always have another day to make up for it, but such is not always the case.

Among these three, the third purpose is considered the most important for the Stoics. It is easy to appreciate something that is new, for example, a new mobile phone. However, as time passes, it also becomes easy for such appreciation to wane, which even affects the level of one's happiness. You simply get used to its existence that it appears to lose its original value. Psychologists refer to this attitude as a hedonistic adaptation. By practicing negative visualization, you get to counter the effects of this hedonistic adaptation. Instead, you learn to appreciate things again more fully. Of course, this practice is not limited to material things alone. In fact, a more important use of this exercise is with your loved ones or people who are important to you.

Of course, it is not suggested that you practice this for a long time. Once a day or once every two days would be enough. Take note that you engage in this kind of visualization in order to learn to see the meaning of what you have and appreciate the true value of anything and everything. Although it may make you sad in the process, its true goal is to make you realize the importance of what you have.

You might be wondering: Does this really work? Different individuals tried this exercise and the outcome also had different results. Some were able to appreciate the value of something or someone that is important to them even more, while others did not appear to feel any changes, even emotionally, after the exercise. Therefore, it can be said that this exercise depends on the individual who is applying it. The reason why others failed completely may have been because they were fully convinced that they were merely imagining things — that they were not real. However, those who participated well and took the steps more seriously were able to feel the amazing effect of the visualization even within the first few minutes of the exercise.

Take note that there is no hard and fast rule as to how long you should engage in this exercise. The important thing is for you to *feel* it, internalize it as if it were real until you realize the true meaning of what you have.

Self-denial

This practice may not be appealing to most people. The Stoics also practice self-denial. This is where you deny yourself some pleasure from time to time. For example, if you like smoking a cigarette after a meal, then you should control yourself and not light a cigarette after your next meal. Of course, this is only temporary. It does not mean absolutely removing whatever gives you a sense of pleasure.

So, why should you practice self-denial? According to the Stoics, by denying yourself of things of pleasure from time to time, you get to appreciate their value more fully. This is similar to negative visualization; however, in this case, you literally experience being deprived of something that you want. A study conducted at Stanford Institute shows that practicing self-denial can also help strengthen your willpower, which is an important element to succeed in life.

Indifference

It bears stressing that the concept of indifference to Stoicism is different from the normal notion of being indifferent. It is worth noting that Stoics are not indifferent. Therefore, they do not practice an unloving or uncaring behavior to others. They are not bad people. The common view of indifference refers to things like money. Some people think that since life means so much more than money, then you should be indifferent to money. Although Stoicism also considers this part of being indifferent, they also acknowledge the value of money. In fact, they can even be grateful for it. To the Stoics, indifference simply means that something is neutral. This means that it can be used for good or bad. Instead of understanding it as being indifferent, consider it being "neutral."

There is also the Stoic concept of apatheia. It is unfortunate that some people consider this as being the same with indifference. This is wrong. It should be noted that apatheia does not mean apathy. Rather, it refers to a state of having no irrational emotional states. To the Stoics, you need to be rational with your emotions. In the modern world, however, people usually think of emotion as something that is not rational. In Stoicism, an emotional only becomes irrational when you are not able to control it.

A key point to remember about the concept of indifference is that true Stoics also concern themselves with external things like money. Like any other human being, they also enjoy building a good relationship with people. However, a significant difference that they have is that their virtue and happiness do not depend upon the presence or absence of someone or something.

"Let it make no difference to thee whether thou art cold or warm, if thou art doing thy duty.

Focus on the positive things

"Dwell on the beauty of life. Watch the stars, and see yourself running with them."
—Marcus Aurelius, Meditations

A trick to appreciating things more completely

"Do not indulge in dreams of having what you have not, but reckon up the chief of the blessings you do possess, and then thankfully remember how you would crave for them if they were not yours."
— *Marcus Aurelius, Meditations*

Define what wealth means to you

The modern world is good at convincing people to want more and desire more material wealth. In fact, it is not uncommon these days to judge a person by the amount of wealth that he possesses. However, Stoicism encourages that you should not allow the world to dictate the meaning or need to acquire wealth in your life.

The teaching of Stoicism on wealth is similar to the Buddhist teaching of the empty cup. Imagine that there are two cups. One cup is a large cup, while the other one is a small cup. Now, if you pour water into these cups, they will soon be overflowing with water. Can you say which cup is fuller?

To the Stoics, the cup is like your wants. The more wants that you have, the bigger is your cup, and it will need more water for it to be full. However, if you can learn to control your desires and only focus on those things that matter, then it will be easy to fill your cup. In fact, it will be overflowing with water which symbolizes wealth.

You might be wondering: If there is nothing wrong with getting a large cup, then why not? Well, there is also a problem with having a large cup. Having so many wants and possessions tend to divide your time and attention. For example, if you have so many clothes, you will need more time to choose which dress you are going to wear. Also, as they say, you can be a jack of all trades, yet a master of none. To the Stoics, you need to control and decide what wealth really means to you. Do not let it depend on what the modern world promotes through the media. It is sad to say, but it is the media that makes people feel more stressed out and unsatisfied with their life. They tend to promote stuff that is not only worth so much more than their value, but also make people become more mundane than spiritual or philosophical.

To the Stoics, there is nothing wrong with wealth. In fact, the Stoics know how to appreciate wealth. Also, there is nothing wrong with aspiring to be wealthy.

However, you should learn how to be satisfied with what you have and to not make wealth the master of your life.

It is also not good to depend your happiness on wealth. After all, material possessions can come and go at any time. For example, that new and expensive handbag that you bought yesterday may be stolen from you today. Even if your business is doing really well today does not guarantee that no competitor can beat you in the future. Of course, this does not mean that you should not focus and work on gaining material wealth, but you need to control it. More importantly, you need to understand just how these things of value really mean to you.

"Wealth consists not in having great possessions, but in having few wants." – *Epictetus*

"It is not the man who has too little, but the man who craves more, that is poor." —*Seneca*

Set goals for yourself

Man usually has goals in life. To the Stoics, it is important that you be aware of these goals. You then have to set yourself in the direction that will lead you to your goals. Of course, for this to be possible, you need to know what your goals are.

It is important that you know what your goals in life are. Otherwise, you can get easily controlled by many external factors. This can make you live a life that you do not want to live. Hence, it is of utmost importance that you know what you want in life. Especially today where most people are controlled by the dictates of society and direction set by the media, it is easy to get lost in this world.

"If a man knows not what harbor he seeks, any wind is the right wind." —*Seneca*

Happiness is a choice

To the Stoics, happiness or misery is a matter of state of one's mind. Do not forget that happiness is a choice that you can always make. Also, if you think that you are so miserable, then you are. Hence, it is important to control your state of mind. Of course, this kind of happiness is not blind but includes positive actions. Stoicism does not rely on self-delusion but is an active approach to life.

You always have a choice in everything in life. It is then up to you whether you choose what can lead you to happiness or misery. Happiness is also a matter of dealing with misery. For example, if you suddenly become blind permanently, it would be normal for you to feel very sad. However, it is up to you on how you will deal with such misery. Will you allow yourself to be stuck in such misery for a long time or will you gather every strength that you have and move forward with your life? This is a choice that you need to make. As such, being in misery is a choice just as being happy is also a matter of making a choice or decision.

"A man's as miserable as he thinks he is." —Seneca

Be cheerful

A true Stoic has a sense of cheerfulness. This kind of joy, of course, is not delusional but proceeds from being satisfied with one's inner state. Just like the example above, sometimes you may not have a choice as to what happens in your life. However, you always have a choice on how you would deal with it. How you react is something that is under your control, as well as how you view a particular situation. Hence, the question: "Is the cup half full or half empty?" You decide.

The practices of Stoicism will make it easy for a man to be cheerful even during such times when his strength is being tested. Another benefit of maintaining such cheerfulness is that people tend to think and function better when cheerful. However, when the mind is stressed out, then it can be difficult to come up with amazing ideas.

With Stoicism, you will be more in control of your thoughts and emotions. You will also appreciate better the things that you have in your life. All these help you to remain cheerful at all times. Also, a follower of this path is not controlled by pain or pleasure. You will learn how to appreciate things as they are and be satisfied with everything. Also, by improving the quality of your thoughts, you will be more able to exercise a more cheerful personality.

"A man thus grounded must, whether he wills or not, necessarily be attended by constant cheerfulness and a joy that is deep and issues from deep within, since he finds delight in his own resources, and desires no joys greater than his inner joys."
—Seneca, The Stoic Philosophy of Seneca: Essays and Letters

Chapter 3: Moving Forward

Now that you have learned the different teachings of Stoicism, you already have a good foundation of what Stoicism is. However, the only way to truly realize what it means to be a Stoic is to continuously live the teachings and principles of Stoicism.

Be a Stoic

When people talk about Stoicism, they often think about it as something that belongs to the ancient time, and that Stoics no longer exist. By now, you should already understand that Stoicism is very much alive in the modern world, and there are still Stoics out there. Is it not amazing that although the main figures of Stoicism did not enjoy having a big audience the spirit of Stoicism remains alive? People die — but ideas, especially those that speak the truth, are immortal. So long as people learn and accept the ideas of Stoicism, and as long as they put into practice these ideas, then Stoicism will not die.

Now, it is up to you to decide to be a Stoic or not. Luckily, there is no requirement that you take a particular course or undergo a special form of training to be a Stoic. Rather, you should live as a Stoic. This means that you put the teachings of Stoicism into positive actions. For example, when your colleague gives you a bad remark, you can apply the Stoic's teachings of postponing your reaction. This will allow you to see things more clearly and not be conquered by destructive emotions. Being a true Stoic, nothing outside of you should be able to take away your virtue and happiness. You are indifferent to pain and pleasure, but you know how to appreciate them at the same time.

If you want to be happy, or at least be happier, then why not give Stoicism a try? All you need to do is to make a decision to do so and start applying its teachings in your day-to-day life. Even just for once, why not try and experience what it means to be a true Stoic? After all, the only way to truly understand the meaning of Stoicism is by living it.

Also, you do not have to accept everything that Stoicism teaches. Many people these days learn from various traditions and only absorb those that they like. If you want, you can also do the same. Although, logically speaking, there seems to be nothing wrong with accepting the core values that Stoicism teach since they are all positive in nature.

Moving forward, you should remember the words of Epictetus: "First say to yourself what you would be, and then do what you have to do." By now, you should already have the right knowledge to pursue the path of Stoicism. Should you decide to embrace this path, then you should take action and "do what you have to do."

What to expect

When you first let go and jump into Stoicism, you can expect to feel two things at the same time: a joy knowing that you are now living a meaningful path, as well as hardship due to the challenges along the journey. Now, it is worth noting that it is not easy to be a Stoic. In fact, simply the teaching where you delay responding to a negative stimulus is not as easy as it seems. This is true, especially when you are irritated already. Hence, do not expect the path to be easy. After all, anything that is worth pursuing in the world is never without difficulty. Do not worry; the more you learn and practice the teachings of Stoicism, and the longer you stay on the path, the easier it will be.

On a positive note, you may experience for the first time, a sense of indescribable happiness. After all, it is always a joy to live a virtuous life. Also, it feels good to see and feel that you are improving as a person and that you are working on something is meaningful.

Be open to change

Once you decide to apply the Stoic teachings in your life, then you should also be open to change. Many people are afraid of change. This is because change is usually accompanied of being outside of your comfort zone. However, this should not be considered a bad thing, especially if the change that you seek is of a positive nature. Therefore, be open to change, expect that Stoicism will change you as a person.

Now, there are people who do not like the idea of change simply because they are too concerned about what other people may think of them. If you are one of these people then remember the Stoic teaching of not being too concerned about what other people think of you. After all, Stoicism is a positive path that encourages positive energies like happiness, peace, and love. Hence, you do not have to worry about turning into something that you may not like. Take note, however, that it takes effort to change, and breaking a habit takes time. However, the good news is that it is possible to change, especially changing for the better.

Learn from your mistakes

You can expect to commit some mistakes from time to time. There is a big difference between knowing what to do and actually doing it. The Stoic discipline may not be as easy as it seems. When you commit mistakes (which you will), you should learn to be kind to yourself. It is not easy to learn how to exercise control over your own mind and emotions. Instead of feeling bad, you should admit that you have committed a mistake and reflect on it. Remember that doing regular reflection is a part of Stoicism. Accordingly, you should reflect each time you fail to follow the teachings of the path, and understand what made you act in a wrong way. Of course, when you do this, you need to be open to making some adjustments or changes in order for you to avoid committing the same mistake. There is always something important that you can learn with every mistake. The important thing is that you do not give up and that you continue to learn. Just like in anything else in life, knowledge and continuous practice are important to achieve perfection and success.

Stay humble

A common mistake committed by those who pursue Stoicism or any other path/philosophy is being arrogant or self-centered. Take note that even if the people around you do not know what Stoicism is, it does not mean that you have a higher level of philosophy or spirituality than them. Sometimes when you read too much of these things, it is easy to feel as if you stand on a higher level than other people. This is a common blunder that you should avoid. Therefore, it is important for you to stay humble. This is one of the benefits of committing mistakes. Each time you commit a mistake, it is another reason for you to be humble. Also, do not underestimate other people. There are many people out there who have no idea what Stoicism is but are able to live their lives better than those people who claim to be Stoics. Again, reading all the books on Stoicism is not enough to make you a Stoic. To live as a Stoic, you need to develop a courageous and kind heart, mind, and soul.

As you continue to learn and mature as a Stoic, it will also be normal for you to feel as if you are much better than others. Take note that this is normal, but it is not considered good. Boosting one's ego is not a key to happiness. On the contrary, being too egotistical would be very much counterproductive to your purpose. Therefore, even if it is true that you have a better philosophical or spiritual level than most people, it is best for you to remain humble. A saint does not say to another saint that he is holier than him (the other saint) or the others. A saint is a saint because of the way he lives. In the same way, as a Stoic, you should live a life of virtue and wisdom, without having to compete with others as to who is a better Stoic for such thing does not exist. You only have to prove yourself to yourself. Proving yourself to others is usually a sign of immaturity. Stay humble.

Continuous study

Although this book lays down the important teachings of Stoicism, do not content yourself just with this book. Do not forget that knowledge plays an important role on Stoicism. Therefore, take the time to read and study the works of the different Stoics, especially those of Marcus Aurelius, Epictetus, and Seneca. You can find their works or writings online. It is also nice to visit the bookstore and get more books about Stoicism. The more you know about Stoicism, the more teachings you can apply in your life.

If you can, it would be good to join groups on Stoicism and also meet people who share the same interest. The collective consciousness that you can get for being a group can help in your development. Just be sure to mingle with those who are truly serious and passionate about living as a Stoic.

Also, it is a good habit to ponder on each of the Stoic teachings. There are simply many new learnings and wisdom that you can draw from the words of the masters. Therefore, it is a good practice to devote some time for reflecting on the teachings of the Stoics on a regular basis. For example, there are many valuable lessons that you can draw from the basic teaching that you should learn to exist in the present moment. Another example is how do you really make every moment count? Of course, such things may depend upon your present situation in life. The good news is that all the Stoic teachings are always applicable. They are universal teachings that you can follow regardless of the time or age, as well as your own status in life.

Practice

Living a life as a Stoic is not that easy, just as it is not easy to be a true Christian. You can expect to face countless of challenges and temptations to abandon the path; but, it bears stressing that it is through these hardships that you can grow better as a Stoic.

Make it a point to practice the different teachings of Stoicism on a day-to-day basis. For example, every evening, you should spend some time to reflect on what happened during the day. You can also spend some time practicing negative visualization. Of course, Stoicism means more than a body of practices, but is a way of life. You can use its teachings when you deal with problems, as well as how you deal with those around you.

It is through regular practice of the teachings of Stoicism that one becomes and matures as a Stoic. Do not rush the process. Learning takes time, and change also takes time. Do not worry; every effort that you make is never wasted. Just as anyone who desires to learn to truly live as a Stoic needs to devote himself to continuous study, such must be accompanied by continuous practice. In fact, the actual practice or application can be considered more important than the study itself.

According to Seneca, there are two important ingredients to happiness: Wisdom (right knowledge) and virtue. Of course, these two unite themselves in the form of positive actions. Do not forget that Stoicism does not just exist in the mind or in the realm of ideas. It has to exist as an idea or principle that is manifested through positive actions. Of course, the best way to practice Stoicism is to act on its teachings in your everyday life.

Conclusion

Thanks for making it through to the end of this book. We hope it was informative and able to provide you with all of the tools you need to achieve your goals whatever they may be.

The next step is to apply everything that you have learned. Do not forget that the true spirit of Stoicism exists in actual practice. Therefore, do your best to live the Stoic teachings and principles.

Finally, if you found this book useful in any way, a review on Amazon is always appreciated!

Help me improve this book

While I have never met you, if you made it through this book I know that you are the kind of person that is wanting to get better and is willing to take on tough feedback to get to that point. You and I are cut from the same cloth in that respect. I am always looking to get better and I wish to not just improve myself, but also this book. If you have positive feedback, please take the time to leave a review. It will help other find this book and it can help change a life in the same way that it changed yours. If you have constructive feedback, please also leave a review. It will help me better understand what you, the reader, need to make significant improvements in your life. I will take your feedback and use it to improve this book so that it can become more powerful and beneficial to all those who encounter it.

REMEMBER TO JOIN THE GROUP NOW!

If you have not joined the Mastermind Self Development group yet, now is your time! You will receive videos and articles from top authorities in self development as well as a special group only offers on new books and training programs. There will also be a monthly member only draw that gives you a chance to win any book from your Kindle wish list!

If you sign up through this link http://www.mastermindselfdevelopment.com/specialreport you will also get a special free report on the Wheel of Life. This report will give you a visual look at your current life and then take you through a series of exercises that will help you plan what your perfect life looks like. The workbook does not end there; we then take you through a process to help you plan how to achieve that perfect life. The process is very powerful and has the potential to change your life forever. Join the group now and start to change your life!

http://www.mastermindselfdevelopment.com/specialreport

You will also love these other great titles from Mastermind Self Development!

You will want to check out these other great titles Mastermind Self Development. All available in the Kindle store or you can just click on covers below.

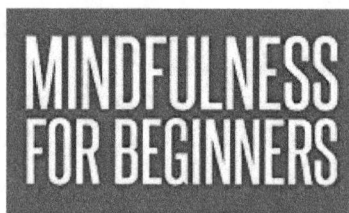

http://viewbook.at/mindfulnesscombo

http://mybook.to/minimalism50tricks

You can also find these titles by searching them in the [Kindle store](#) on Amazon.